THE MAGICAL RED FOX

A MAGICAL STORY

ASHIRVAD A. NAIR

ISBN 979-888521892-4

Contents

Elijah Asleep

CHAPTER ONE

The Magical Red Fox

It was a night. Elijah couldn't sleep.

Elijah : Oh, Dad! I forgot to say I saw a red fox on the way back to home from school!

    Dad : That's great! How was the fox like?

    Elijah : It was **red** and **scary**.

    Dad : Oh! I know a story about a red and scary fox!

    Elijah : Can you tell me?

    Dad : Yes! But promise to sleep after I tell you.

    Elijah : Okay, dad!

    Once there was a red fox. It looked red and scary. It lived in a green forest.

    There were other wild animals like lions, elephants, giraffes. They all lived happily.

    There were two leaders - A lion and the red fox.

    Soon, a rumor was spread that the fox flies up to the sky to find prey.

    No one knew if this was true. The fox did not know about this rumor.

    But, no one decided to stay up and ruin their night to see if the fox could fly.

CHAPTER TWO

Flying Fox

One day, an elephant stayed up at night to see if the fox could fly. He was really sleepy but he wanted to see if the fox could fly. He saw that the fox was sleeping. However, the elephant decided to wait. After a long time of waiting, the elephant slept. Yet, the fox wasn't seen flying to the sky looking for prey.

The next day, the elephant was displeased he didn't see the fox flying.

The rumor spread each day. The fox finally found out about this rumor and was irritated.

Many days later, everyone stayed up at night to see if the fox could fly. After a while, it did appear that the fox did fly to find prey. Everyone was shocked by this incident! A magical fox, alas!

Just like that, the fox revealed that he could fly.

He could soar through the clouds.

CHAPTER THREE

Flying And Soaring

" The fox can fly! "
Said everyone. The fox could actually fly.
"Flying, Soaring! It would be so fun if I could fly"
Said the elephant.

Elijah asleep

Like that, Elijah was finally asleep in his bed.

Dad : Oh, Elijah. You're my little boy...

$\overline{oo}$

THE END $\overline{oo}$

ᴑᴑ ᴑᴑ ᴑᴑ ᴑᴑ

ᴑᴑ ᴑᴑ ᴑᴑ ᴑᴑ

o͞o

o͞o

oͦoͦ

oͦoͦ